You Can Only Be
BETTER

Secrets On How To Lead A More Fulfilling Life

SYED MUHAMMAD ABU BAKAR

PARTRIDGE
A Penguin Random House Company

To order additional copies of this book, contact
Toll Free 800 101 2657 (Singapore)
Toll Free 1 800 81 7340 (Malaysia)
orders.singapore@partridgepublishing.com

www.partridgepublishing.com/singapore

Contents

Preface

By holding fast to the motto of **You Can Only Be Better,** human beings can achieve the impossible.

If we had decided that we can never surpass our limits, we would have never achieved flight let alone walked on the moon. The title of this book is a declaration of self-improvement. Self-improvement that is limitless. Self-improvement that is not reserved just for the experts—but the common man.

By affirming that you can only be better, you are making a commitment. A firm commitment to improve yourself, regardless of circumstances. When I first created **The Green Apple Project,** I wanted to educate youths that no matter the situation, no matter how difficult their current problems are, they can only BE better. Not 'get better', but BE better.

Because success is not by achieving something, it is when you **BECOME** someone. Likewise, to improve your situation is not to change what is outside but to change what is inside. 'Being' better means that you as an individual must improve **YOURSELF** first, before your situation can become better.

Syed Muhammad Abu Bakar
Creator, Lead Inspirator
Specializing in Life Transition and Managing Adversity

Continuous self-improvement

Secondly, the word 'better' implies that your condition can never be stagnant. The word 'better' will take away the limits or the 'ceiling' in your mind which stops you from growing. When we embark on the journey to improve ourselves, the last thing you want to do is put a limit to yourself. Your success depends on how high you believe you can be. And if you want to be the 'best', you won't be the best for long because there will always be people like you who are rising. Eventually they will surpass you and you lose your position at the top.

Life is not about competition. Life is about continuous self-improvement. You don't seek to beat others, you seek to beat yourself. You grow and keep growing because you believe in 'better', and don't stop at 'best'.

About This Book

I wrote the first manuscript for this book in 2013 when my family and I were on vacation in Indonesia. My team and I had just formed The Green Apple Project and we were working hard to grow the newborn company. The place I visited was so *zen* and tranquil that I found myself sitting down and writing for hours about my life and the lessons which made me who I am. It was then that I placed the intention to collect my ideas into a book.

I wanted this book to be simple and relatable. And I wanted to be as sincere as I could in writing it. The contents of this book is 10 lessons on how you, the reader, can put to practice immediately to improve yourself and your life. You can start at any chapter you like and read it in any fashion you find most comfortable. I don't believe in coming up with a structured, one-size-fits-all formula for success, because quite frankly, it doesn't exist. Success comes differently to all human beings, yet the fundamental principles are the same.

Therefore I want you to feel free in reading and applying the ideas in this book to how you deem fit. No sequences, no structure, just ideas. Study these ideas and apply them in your daily life. Along the way, you will make certain discoveries on your own and craft out a success system which will work best for you.

I believe the book can be related to people from all walks of life. I would however recommend this book to be for youths aged 13, all the way up to adults. I'm not a technical person neither am I a learned researcher of sorts, so you can expect little to no use of jargon in this book. My editor told me I write as if I am speaking to you directly. Well, I am but an ordinary guy, and this book is meant for the ordinary reader who wants to live an extraordinary life.

The Era of Problems

People of this era face a common problem—we think too much. As a result, we become overwhelmed with our problems. The problem is not our problems, the problem is WE FOCUS TOO MUCH on our problems! We complain about our problems. We gossip about other people's problems. And we go looking for more problems when we can't solve our current ones!

This book is not to address your problems. This book is meant to address SOLUTIONS. The message I want to really remind you, the reader, is that no matter what problems you are facing, trust me, there are about 6 billion other people facing similar problems as you. At the end of the day, what sets you apart from everyone else is that you have made the decision to focus on SOLUTIONS, and be a better person than you are today. Your solutions may not come today, not tomorrow, not even the week after. But what's important, is that you have started looking for it. Eventually, you will succeed in finding it.

I hope you benefit as much as possible from reading my book. You can only be better.

Acknowledgements

First and foremost, I would like to thank my beloved wife—Fitri Aisyiah—and my three beautiful and loving sons who were patient with me at the lowest points in my life and who never doubted me.

My brothers and companions Hyder Muhammad Taufik and Saiful Reduwan for being the go-to guys and just awesome partners to team up with. They were the brains behind the meteoric success of The Green Apple Project and I truly appreciate the friendship we forged on this journey together.

I'd also like to thank and appreciate all my friends and the society at large—because I've learnt so much from the stories shared by everyday people who inspire me one way or another. When they go to me for advice I end up learning more from them rather than the other way around.

I want to thank the following successful individuals whose stories and advice have made a significant difference to my life:

Mr Malek Mattar, Mdm Kader Beevi, Mr Mohamed Nassir, Dr Azizan Osman, Haji Mohd Asri Ahmad and Abang Abu Abuayubul Ansari

Without the guidance and wisdom of my mentors, I would not be the person who I am today.

Chapter 1:
Say YES! To A More Fulfilling Life

Becoming Better Starts With You

Consider the following questions. Ask yourself, **what are your dreams and what exactly do you need to be happy in life**?

How much time did you spend starting projects but never finishing them?

Have you wished to begin new resolutions but never got down to starting because you doubt you would be able to do it?

That's exactly the problem. **You had already thought you CANNOT do it even before you started**!

The fact is the reason you cannot do what you wish to do is because you have successfully convinced yourself that you can't and will never be able to do it. It does nothing but drain your confidence to achieve anything.

Do you recall a time when someone said to you "Hey, why not try your hand in doing business?" For most people, chances are your answer would have been 'NO' before you even gave it much thought. That was it. You've decided for yourself that you cannot do it.

Begin By Saying 'YES!'

That, my friend, is you first challenge: do not be afraid to face your fears by saying 'YES'. I am not saying that you say 'YES' and immediately dive head-first into something and get burned. Seek knowledge and skills in that particular field you've always wanted to try or interests you. Your passion is not enough. Equipping yourself in specialized skills and knowledge will give you a greater advantage.

Did you know that once upon a time I had absolutely no clue on how to write books and I even hated reading books. And yet here I am writing a book to share my ideas and experiences.

So my friends, do yourself a favour and **stop denying yourself of opportunities**. The next time someone asks you to try something new, try answering this way: "That sounds fantastic! Why don't you share your ideas and let's see how we can make it happen." instead of saying "No, sorry, I'm not interested". This way you will open yourself up to a world of new ideas and opportunities for yourself. Yes, you may not end up doing that particular project or activity but it can lead you to even more new ideas and you become more creative. By immediately saying 'NO', you are hindering yourself from discovering new ideas, people and opportunities which may benefit you.

This should be the first step you take to create a positive transition in yourself. It is simple so live by the Nike slogan and just do it. **Things will never start to change unless you first do something about it**. Many success stories we know starts with the person in subject being a failure but they never give up. They take a step back, re-strategize and come back stronger while avoiding all the mistakes they had previously made.

Many of us face the challenge of having to deal with fear and loss of confidence every time we experience failure. Instead of moving forward despite our failures, we decide to quit pursuing our dream altogether. In life we must have the courage to accept failure, or we will never experience success. It is the harsh reality that only through failure you will understand what it truly means to be successful. Not just any success, but SWEET success—the lasting satisfaction and joy which you will cherish for the rest of your life.

However, my friend, I have to caution you: it is going to be tough. I am afraid you have no choice but to push through it if you really want to be successful. **Take the first step and keep going because eventually you will see the light at the end of the tunnel.** Yes, you will see it if you BELIEVE and have FAITH in yourself.

When you have faith in your success, you will attract to yourself nothing but success. Our minds are powerful satellites, sending out signals of success when we are thinking about success. Hence you become successful. Likewise if you want to be unsuccessful, just focus on 'un-success' and you will send out signals of 'un-success', therefore attracting the forces of 'un-success' to yourself. As the famous line goes, may the force be with you!

Positive Versus Negative

Speaking of forces, let me give you a simple explanation on what we need to remain POSITIVE all the time and not allow the NEGATIVE energy rule over our mind.

I believe everyone is familiar with the symbol for POSITIVE (+) and the symbol of NEGATIVE (-). You will agree that these two symbols represent addition and subtraction respectively? With every POSITIVE (+ve) object your hold in your mind, you will begin to add more of such things into your life: money, health, confidence and whatever we desire. But when our mind is full of nothing but NEGATIVE (-ve) objects, I can assure you everything that you desire, have or achieve will eventually be taken away from you.

So my friends, I can assure you that if you knew the journey of success would not be all smooth sailing, many will not hesitate to forget about it altogether. That is why not many are considered successful. But I believe and cannot stress enough that if you take action on what I am sharing with you here in this book, not only will you succeed but you will lead a more FULFILLING life.

Before I go to the next chapter, remember that life is abundant and there is enough of everything for everyone. One key to lead a more fulfilling life is to not be greedy. Ask yourself if you are able to finish a whole cow? Most of us would stop at just two plates as we only have limited space to fill our bellies. Be thankful for what you already have, and you will immediately feel more fulfilled with your life.

Chapter 2:
Moving Forward In Transition

Overcoming Resistance

In the process of transition, rest assured there will be resistance. But know that there is nothing we cannot overcome.

A common form of resistance is that you will have other people judging and criticizing you. Trust me, this may not come from anyone but your own family and friends. This may force you to make some difficult choices.

I am saying this not to scare you but it is because I have gone through it personally. Along the way to where I am now, I have lost some friends. As sad as I am about it, I have no choice but to move on in my life. I am seeking happiness, fulfilment and success in my life and plus, my beloved wife and children are depending on me.

I even had to struggle with the relationships I have with some family members who were persistently negative of anything that I wished to do. For example, I told them I wanted to go into business and all I got from them were all the reasons I wouldn't make it in business. They argued that I was too stupid to do business and that there was no security in running a business. Plus every time I expressed the desire to make a transition in my life, they told me not to bother and just accept the life you've been given and be happy about it.

Being grateful does not mean that if you have a crappy job, you need to just suck it up and stick with it. **Being grateful means doing what you are doing while finding ways to make it better than it is now**.

You need to know that every single experience is a learning experience. And in the course of pursuing your true passion, you will have to go through moments which you may not enjoy. Hence I use the word *transition*. **Be grateful for ALL experiences in your life and if you are consistently positive about them, you can learn much from them.** Be assured that all experiences serve you until you are ready to claim that ultimate success which you desire.

<u>Keeping Positive Company</u>

Though I did not completely sever the ties I have with family members who responded in negativity, my experiences with them did make me more wary of others like them. We must be strong enough to take negativity, pick ourselves up when we fall and continue to focus on our goals no matter what. I have to admit that although I've lost some friends, I never regretted my loss because then I don't have to deal with their negative comments and discouragement anymore.

Today, all my friends are very positive and encouraging by nature. While I was once someone who never read any books (unless I had no choice), I never thought that one day I would actually be writing one! All this is possible because I had the support and encouragement of friends who believed I could do what I am doing now.

For our other friends who are unsupportive or are constantly discouraging, do not hate them but forgive them, so that in turn, you may be forgiven. **Be sympathetic on them for they have yet to see the truth about what is life is all about.**

Life is about service and we've yet to see that we are lacking the need to show service to others in our life. We focus RECEIVING but forget about GIVING. We focus on HATING but forget about LOVING. We focus on DESTROYING but forget about BUILDING. We were born free of all hatred, free of all disease, free of all sins, free from ignorance and even free from stupidity. Yet we contract all of them when we grow older. So can you see that we have no one to blame but ourselves? We've yet to realize what we've done.

We've made some wrong choices in our lives but that is perfectly fine because we didn't know any better! You can't avoid inexperience. You can never differentiate between right and wrong without some form of education. We acted the way we did because of the way we were raised. **The first step to positive change is the awareness that you CAN change.**

Hence I want to put forth the fact that it is never too late to make that transition in ourselves. As long as we are still breathing, there is an opportunity to make a difference to our lives.

Positivity is like a ripple effect, it has to begin from that core where the pebble touches the surface of the water. So YOU, my friend, must be that core. Be consistently positive and you will radiate ripples of positivity to others. **Do not wait for others to give you positivity, be a source of positivity yourself.**

The Adventurer's Checklist for Transition

Transition is phase in life which requires taking small steps, patience, and faith that one day we may reach the peak of success. Imagine that you have decided to climb Mount Everest and your goal is to stand on its peak. You don't just pack up, leave and start climbing! There is a process you need to follow and you need to be well-prepared. Forget Mount Everest, before ANY long journey, you need to have a checklist to ensure that you are well-equipped with everything you need to reach your destination. Here is my checklist:

1. You need a mentor to guide you through the challenges that lie ahead—whether physically, mentally, emotionally or spiritually.
2. You need to be able to manage your finances well as there will be things that you need to buy along the way to support your cause.
3. You need to be ready to learn new skills that would be vital to your survival on your journey.
4. You need to learn to quickly adapt to a new environment. For example, the climb is not the only challenge you may face. You will have to deal with the harsh conditions such as the altitude, the rocky paths, the freezing temperatures and many more unexpected difficulties.
5. You need to be mentally prepared. Showing gratitude and having strong belief and faith is a good way to start.
6. You need to be ready to do more of what you don't like and do less of what you like.
7. You need to have a positive attitude towards transition and see every experience as an opportunity to learn something new.

YOU CAN ONLY BE BETTER

8. You need to be willing to deflate your ego and readily accept advice from your mentor even if you do not like it as sometimes what you dislike may turn out to be good for you (. . . like vegetables).

Before I conclude this chapter, arm yourself for your transition period with patience as you are about to lay the foundations for creating the life you desire. Dreams are nothing but castles on air—they will always remain a fantasy without the solid foundations to turn them into reality.

Chapter 3:
The Value of Giving

Life Is About Service

Many of us are so obsessed with creating wealth that it becomes a sole objective in life. In the process we lose our souls and sense of belonging. We lose touch with the true purpose of living—to be of SERVICE.

Yes, that's right, my friend. We do not only ask ourselves how much wealth we are creating but WHO we are creating the wealth for—for ourselves, or for the greater needs of society. We make a transition not only in our actions, but also make a transition in our INTENTION of creating wealth. We could create wealth for our own selfish purposes or we could choose to do it for our loved ones and those who may need it. **You see my friends—the more you give, the more you will get back.** That is how the universe works—what goes around comes around.

Sometimes what you give may not come back as money, but it may come back as wealth in other forms: health, more time with loved ones, happiness and most importantly, a blessed life. Happiness if shared with others is the most blessed version of happiness. You see, money may help to solve problems in your life, but it is not the reason for your happiness. **Overall happiness is created when you serve to create happiness in others.**

Learn how you can make a difference in others' lives and trust me, you will continuously get more and more. Remember, life is not just about amassing wealth but to give a part of it to those who really need it.

Simple Formula to Make More Money: M-O-N-E-Y

Let me share with you something inspired to me by my beloved son Syed Muhammad Umar. We were just chatting one day about what I am doing and he suggested a fantastic acronym for making money as simply: M-O-N-E-Y. I was so impressed by his great idea I had to share it with you in this book. Here is the formula:

M: Manage—Learn how to manage your money. Money can be easy to make but much harder to keep. To be wealthy you need to be an excellent money manager.

O: Opportunities—Train yourself to see opportunities to make money because they can be found just everywhere if you are open-minded enough.

N: New Ideas—Value all your ideas. Be creative. Don't assume your current skills cannot lead to a profitable idea which could in turn lead you to riches.

E: Engage—Start engaging yourself in networking activities. Attend seminars, workshops, or any networking session where you can connect with like-minded individuals and build collaborative relationships.

Y: Y must I buy from you?—That is the question you need to ask yourself first. You must take into consideration not just why other people would want to buy your products and services but also buy your TRUST. Clients who trust you are so much easier to do business with. And they also serve as your own (free!) marketing agents.

(I would like to thank my beloved son Syed Muhammad Umar who gave me the inspiration on how to make money. I would not have thought of it if he hadn't said anything. Well done, my son!)

<u>Start Giving Today</u>

Giving and sharing does not necessarily mean money. You could give and share things like knowledge, ideas, food and advice. You could help others by giving them a job. You could lend a helping hand. The least you could do is SMILE, and that alone can brighten someone's day.

My friends, if you want to be truly happy and successful, you have to start giving. If you feel that giving will make you poor then you are thinking from mind-set of poverty—which will only make you poorer and unhappy. But if you think from a mind-set of abundance—you will find that you will be returned with much, much more than what you initially gave away. What goes around comes around. Hoard all your money today, and trust me, you'll lose it all before you know it.

Start giving. The law of attraction is absolute. The more you give, the more you get. Be generous and attract generosity.

Chapter 4:
Writing Your Success Story

Being Ready For Success

In preparation for a major transition, you have to be ready. And here you are thinking—be ready for what?

Two things you need to be ready for. First, you need to be ready to LEARN NEW THINGS. You need to reprogram your mind by telling yourself that you need to be on the lookout for new ideas, be creative and take initiative. This first thing is pretty obvious to make a successful transition so I will not go too deep into it. The second thing you need to be ready for is much more important but not many of us are aware of it. The second thing you must be ready for is JUDGEMENT. Yes, your friends and even your closest loved ones will start to judge you when they see changes in you. Hence you must be strong at this early stage of transition.

The reason for this is because they have yet to accept the idea of a 'new you' and you cannot blame them. Maybe there were times in the past when you said you will change but you failed to do so. The key here is you need to know that the one who benefits from your change is YOU! **No one else will benefit more from your changes than you.** The others can only be happy for you but they have their own lives and dreams to pursue.

Moving up phases in life, making positive changes at your own pace and becoming better than you were yesterday— that is what I call transition. When you come across difficult moments in your life, do not feel sad or dejected. Instead, look into the mirror, state your name and say: I CAN ONLY BE BETTER. I DESERVE TO BE HAPPY AND LEAD A FULFILLING LIFE.

Again, I stress, it is not going to be easy. Some days you may have to go cold turkey, so just hang in there. When I go through my own difficult changes in life, only God knows how much blood, sweat and tears I shed. But when I look at the faces of my wife and sons, I tell myself that I MUST be better for them. Look at your loved ones as a source of inspiration and with that in mind, I am sure you do not wish to let them down at all cost.

The Three 'M's of Success

Here are three keys which I believe is critical for us to understand at the beginning of any success journey:

1. Mentor
2. Mistakes
3. Money Management

No matter what field you're in or what area of life you're looking to improve, you need a MENTOR to guide you. As we learn and grow we have to be accepting of the MISTAKES we make because without them, we can never attain the next level. Thirdly, it is an absolute must that you learn some basic MONEY MANAGEMENT.

The reason successful people live in financial freedom is because they know not just how to make money but to effectively KEEP it. Without the wisdom to manage your money, then you can potentially set yourself up to eventually lose it all. Having money is an awesome side effect of success and can bring you joy and satisfaction, but if you don't understand the money game it can just as easily bring you a fourth 'M'—MISERY.

The fact is: money is NOT the root of all problems—the FAILURE to manage money is the root of all problems. Before we set off on a journey to develop ourselves, be aware of these 3 'M's and you will be well on your way to a more fulfilling life.

My friend, the universe is not out there to hurt us, Mother Nature is not out to destroy us and God did not send us here on Earth to torture us. We are sent here to be of SERVICE and the best of all service is service to oneself, our loved ones, the community and God. Everything that we do is a service. No matter how rich we are in our lives, we need to realize that we are not independent and there are others who depend on us.

The Meaning of Being Rich

I mentioned that when we give, we become richer. When I say 'richer' most will think of richer in terms of money. I won't blame you as most of us are programmed to associate 'rich' with 'money'. However you can define rich in so many ways other than wealth. Being rich can mean being in the pink of health, being at peace in the mind and soul, happiness from being with your loved ones, and waking up refreshed every day. It could even mean feeling so blessed and happy each day that you do not need money to make you feel that way.

Money is still important so long as you rule over your money and not let it rule over you. It can be very freeing to know that you always have some spare cash around. And when I say spare I mean lots of it! With money you can make massive difference to your quality of life. Many people go to seminars on wealth creation thinking that they will get rich shortly after attending them. But the reality is that most do not get rich and even lose all their money as they have yet to meet the basic fundamentals of creating wealth. Until you have understood the basics, you will only be running in circles. If you do not possess gratitude, then you will never be rich. When you are showing appreciation for what you have, you will realize how rich you already are.

People tend to believe things only when they see it with their own eyes. I am no different. I had always assumed that I can never be rich. All I saw was problems and that everyone else seemed to have it better. So I began to feel poor, useless and everything else BUT grateful. It was until the day I started showing a little gratitude, things began to change—life was better. If you truly believe you are getting better and have an attitude of gratitude, your condition WILL eventually become better.

<u>The Story of My Past</u>

As a guy who used to avoid reading, I know what it feels to come full circle as I write this book to share with you my journey. Today I regret not starting earlier in my learning journey but I believe everything happens for a reason. I am just thankful it wasn't too late when I started.

The lowest point in my life was a result of making some bad choices with my money. I spiralled into huge debt and one by one, my life collapsed into a series of problems. I got really desperate and found myself lost. I didn't even have enough to feed myself let alone my family, and my illnesses only compounded the problems even further. I shed tears of despair almost every day and sought help from all the wrong places. Reflecting back on those days, I am so grateful my family never gave up on me. Even when we were living in difficulty, my wife remained patient and my sons were obedient.

I was about to give up on life. I contemplated death as I have never felt more helpless. I started blaming everything but myself—one of the gravest mistakes you could ever make. The reason your life never improved is because you failed to improve yourself. Your reality is nothing but an end product of your own thoughts and decisions.

I wallowed in my own self-pity for a long time before certain circumstances eventually forced me to realize that in order to get out of this mess, I NEED to improve myself. I had hit rock bottom, so it was pointless to hold on to my ego any longer. I finally admitted my stupid mistakes, learnt from them, and decided to let go. At that very moment, my life turned around.

Today I am so much better and believe I can only be better. The challenges I faced in the past are different from the challenges I face today. Yet I am undeterred because I am now equipped with a new mindset and outlook of life—I believe I can pull through anything. I believe challenges are there to mould me into a better person in life. No matter what you may be going through at this moment, you can turn your life around. You don't need to have to go through a life-threatening disaster to understand how to be a success. You can start with a switch in your mindset.

If you are feeling scared, anxious or helpless—share your fear with someone. My wife was there but I didn't want to burden her. At my lowest, I grieved and turned to God because I had absolutely no one to turn to. Today I feel that God has lifted me to a much better state in life and I cannot be thankful enough.

I believe by sharing my story I can benefit others by showing that you can always turn your life around. True success is not in turning around your own life but in helping others to turn THEIR lives around. I have dedicated my life to do just that and tasted first-hand the incredible rewards that follow.

Tell yourself that you can be a success, and you can only get better. Do this daily—make 'I Can Only Be Better' your mantra and share your new philosophy with your loved ones.

Chapter 5:
Never Need Your Negative Friends

Change Your Friends, Change Your Life

People who are in debt will continue to be in debt. And until they decide to leave the cycle, they will stay in that cycle. If you want to manage your money well, you need to learn financial management. Similarly if you want to manage your life well, you need to learn to manage POSITIVITY.

One thing's for sure: **if you wish to be a positive person, you'll need to make some sacrifices**. I never said it was going to be easy. If you want to have better experiences in life and be a better person, you're going to have to consider one extremely important sacrifice.

You'll have to consider changing your FRIENDS.

Why? Let me tell you. Have you noticed that all your closest friends have the same or similar interests as you? If you are a gambler, chances are your friends are also gamblers. If you love to gossip, your friends love gossiping as much as you do. And if you think your life is not going anywhere—you'll realize that your friends are facing similar problems as you do. Don't just take my word for it, see it for yourself. Worse part is, the moment you make a public decision to be more positive and share such ideas with your friends—they will be the first to react negatively.

For example, if you are a chronic smoker, you tend to spend your time with people who are smokers themselves. Imagine coming up to them one day and you tell them "Dude, no more. I have decided to QUIT." Trust me, their immediate reaction would be "Dude, yeah right!! If quitting was that easy we would've done it long ago. Here, have another stick." And just like that, you pop the cigarette in your mouth and light it up. Without resolve, it is that easy to be influenced by our friends.

This is the reality. Many smokers find it hard to quit not because of their addiction but because of the people around them. If you are one of these people, I don't blame you. However you must be aware of one thing: **You may not be able to change your friends, but you definitely can change yourself first.**

You may wonder: then what about my loved ones? I can relate to that. The situation gets even trickier when your own family—your spouse, kids or parents—are not supportive of your decision to make that transition in life, to be better. You have to be patient. While they may be unsupportive, you should slowly strive to gain their trust and confidence.

<u>A Strategy for Staying Positive</u>

The fact is, negative energy will always be stronger than positive energy. You've read the stories, you've seen the movies. Evil will always creep up on the Good and triumph momentarily. Yet you always know that if Good persists long enough, Good will always prevails in the end. If you'd take a moment to picture Positive and Negative as two men in combat, Negative appears to be naturally stronger. But they lack the intellect possessed by Positive, who is much more Brains than Brawn. Positive can never win if pit against Negative head-on, but definitely has the advantage if equipped with a BETTER STRATEGY.

To be a more positive individual, you'll need a strategy. The easiest strategy is of course, avoid confrontation altogether. Leave your negative friends who never cease in their blaming and complaints. I'm not telling you to turn them into your enemies, but if you are serious about changing and are taking baby steps towards positive transition, then it is best to begin avoiding them. Just walk away. I did just that and guess what, I am way happier now than before. My life is so much better since then (especially financially!)

You'll need to remember a simple concept about friends. If you treasure their friendship, and they in turn treasure yours, you have to ask them to be supportive of the decisions you make to improve your life. This is critical. **If they continue to be resentful, then they really have no place in your life.** If they are not looking out for you and have no interest in your interests, they're not worth your time. Start looking for friends who are on your side.

Top 10 Friends to Avoid At All Costs

Ever heard of the saying "great minds think alike"? It's absolutely true. Your subconscious mind attracts into your life people who share similar characteristics as you do. **The lesson is that you are a reflection of your closest friends.**

I personally experienced this. The moment I made the clear and definite intention to be a millionaire, I started to realize that I have more rich friends. And I wasn't even a millionaire yet! Now most of the people in my circle are successful millionaires. A significant number of them are philanthropists who I admire and who I desire to emulate.

It's crucial to know the type of people you want to attract in your life. But it's even MORE important to know the type of people to avoid. Unless you start avoiding these venomous people, you'll keep the good ones at bay. Here's my list of Top 10 Friends to Avoid At All Costs . . .

1. The Complainers

They do nothing but talk about the unhappiness in their life. You'll find that they're seldom enjoy themselves, because of their excessive focus for 'what's wrong' instead of 'what's right'.

2. The Whiners

They're pretty much like complainers. Except they sound funnier and annoy the HELL out of you with their constant whining. You can identify them easily because they love to ask 'WHY ME?' They always need a good reason to be better. That's why they never do.

3. The Sore losers

They love to sulk when things aren't going their way. They find ways to put the blame on as many people before they accept responsibility for anything. They blame the world for their bad luck instead of seeing how they can move on.

4. The Huge Egos

They tend to be very comfortable with their success and love to exaggerate their past victories. They love to give advice but feel insulted when given advice.

5. The Jealous

People who envy you will attempt to condemn you in multiple ways. Instead of learning from your example and choose to be better in their own way, they complain, whine and even spread lies about you.

6. The Justifiers

When are given advice on how to improve, Justifiers love to find excuses for why they are who they are.

7. The Find-Faulters

They get a kick of finding other people's flaws . . . and are completely oblivious to their own.

8. The Drifters

They know nothing, wish to remain knowing nothing, and carry on their lives aimlessly.

9. The Poor

I'm not referring to dead-broke poor, I'm referring to people with a poor mentality. They tend to be selfish and annoyingly self-centered.

10. The Ungrateful

Here's the worst of the lot. They only appear when they need something out of you. Once they've gotten what they needed, they leave without hesitation. Such people tend to hurt the most as they may sometimes appear to be at the best of behaviour around you, in an attempt to exploit you.

Sadly, it is common to identify these types of people to be in your own family. In this case, the only reasonable option is to arm yourself with a strong will. Have the discipline and courage to draw the line and set boundaries. **Be prepared to say 'no' when you have to.** If you are a smoker or drinker, make it clear that you have chosen to quit and thank them for their offer. If you're on a diet and they offer you to eat more, then tell them: "If this goes on, I may have to eat you too." (Keep it light with family. But if they are not the type, then go ahead then go ahead and eat them.)

Remember: if you cannot totally avoid certain negative people in your life (i.e family members), there is always a strategy to avoid their negative impact on you. Persist on your journey to be better and the paths will be revealed to you. Trust me. You will attract much better friends into your life and you will feel at ease with these people. Because they too want would want to make their lives better.

Chapter 6:
Healing Wounds With Forgiveness

Freeing Yourself of Inner Pain

You may have heard of the saying 'time will heal all wounds' but in truth, our most painful memories are locked up somewhere deep in our hearts and minds. We may have grown to be immune to the pain, yet the scars still exist in our subconscious minds.

Don't believe me? Think of a time when someone you know said or did something hurtful to you in the past. Do you at times feel the urge to avoid their company? And do you sometimes cringe when you hear their name ... or even someone who has the same name as them? That's enough to prove that the scars have not healed.

So how can we move on in life with all this 'baggage' which continue to weigh us down and affect our experiences?

If you're ready, the best way is to set up a meeting with the people who used to hurt you and find ways to reconcile. But if you're not prepared to, the alternative is to simply see it first in your mind. Visualize yourself speaking to that person. In your mind, tell that person that you have been hurt but now you have decided not to be angry ... and you forgive them.

I need you to understand that you are not doing this for them, but you are doing this for YOU. The process of visualization is enough to release yourself from all the binding hurt you have inside you. Like you, I too have gone through much painful experiences with people in my life. As the years passed, I thought I was doing well but in reality I wasn't. I continued to think about all these people in my life who hurt me and I let it get to my head. I kept to myself and nearly spiralled into a depression. I'm glad I moved on. I did it by assuring myself that the people who used to hurt me are unaware of what they were doing. They don't realize the truth of their actions even though they know people are hurt by them. I pity them because if they don't change, what they are putting out will definitely come back to bite them.

Releasing Toxic Emotions

To move forward in life it is crucial that you release the unseen hurt and hatred you may be holding back inside you. Such emotions are toxic and though you may not realize it, they have an unconscious effect on all the areas of your life: your health, your career and your relationships. If you don't release these negaive forces within you, you will hinder yourself from progressing in any area of life.

You can practice this simple daily affirmation: "I AM FORGIVING. I WILL FORGIVE SO THAT I MAY BE FORGIVEN." Remember if you feel hurt, there may be others who have been hurt by you too. Worse, they may bear grudges against you. So have the courage to forgive so that others will forgive you as well. **The reason we are living in unhappiness, stress and depressive states is because of the negative baggage we continue to carry with us.**

Trust me, after this you will feel better about yourself. You will see that your life will slowly change for the better and you will realize many opportunities start coming your way. **Releasing negativity in your life will make space for more positivity—and positivity attracts opportunity.** So if you are looking for more opportunities, then the answer is clear. Forgive and finally have FREEDOM. That's one thing money can never buy.

Till today I am actively forgiving the people who hurt me, as well as forgiving myself. I say 'actively' because forgiveness is one of the most critical ways to free yourself of negativity, which is something we can never truly escape from. Negativity builds up inside you. If you try to suppress it, it will manifest into your behaviours and will affect the people around you. If you don't want to continuously hurt others, as well as be hurt yourself, you need to practice forgiveness as often as possible. It will be a challenge that will take a lifetime to master, but trust me, it will create wonders in your life you will never have imagined.

Remember this: **what others may do to you, it really DOES NOT matter. What matters is how you handle them.** Whatever they did is of their own accountability. You will not be judged by what they did to you, you will be judged by what YOU are doing. So it is an absolute must to take care of ourselves first for we are responsible for our own reality. We have the power to choose what makes us happy, and what keeps us from being happy.

Chapter 7:
The Time is Now

<u>Turning Time Into Money</u>

People say time is money. If you live by that proverb, I would assume that you attach a value to every day, hour, minute or even second in your life. I used to do so too. But after certain experiences in my life, I've come to realize that the true value of time is measured by the quality of your life. To see time in terms of dollars and cents wouldn't make sense because time cannot be bought nor sold. **Time is an asset if you choose to consciously manage it.** And it becomes a liability if you waste it on doing petty things like quarrelling, arguing, backbiting, complaining, the list goes on.

People love to spend their time on things of low importance. How much time are you spending on things which don't really matter? What matters most is your well-being and your loved ones. How about choosing to focus all your time and energies to improving yourself, upgrading your skills, making better friends, or just doing something worthwhile which will one day lead to something big? There are plenty of ways to use your time more productively.

Stop worrying about your current financial problems and start focusing on SOLUTIONS. You may not have money, but you have TIME. **Start turning your time into money and do something to improve yourself every day.**

Getting The Most Out of 24 Hours

We all have a fixed number of hours a day. 24 hours exactly, of which approximately 7 hours are used up sleeping and 10 hours go into work. That leaves us with about 7 hours left. Most of us have absolutely no idea what goes on in that remaining 7 hours. (Because we're sleeping again, that's why!)

Throughout this book I stress again and again the importance for us to be positive. That's because time is too precious for us to spend in negatively! We know for a fact that time is running out for us and yet we concern ourselves with the lives of others and worry about things that will never happen anyway. By the time you realize it, you will be lying on your deathbed, moments away from meeting your Creator. Are you prepared to go back to Him without realizing your true potential?

There are an infinite number of ways you can think of to make full use of your time. For example when you're at work, you can use time during breaks to call home, say Hi to your spouse and kids . . . or call up your parents or your best friends. Now with technology, you can always settle your bills, mange your side business or reconnect with your old friends via email—all with the use of a smartphone. In commuting between home and work, you can listen to self-improvement audiobooks, read eBooks or watch inspirational videos about successful individuals.

I personally love to learn about the people who have struggled to make a living for themselves and end up amazingly successful. Such stories make me appreciate my own life and give me the motivation I need to push on. I can assure you that you will observe that these people, you will find that they share a similar trait: they all manage their time wisely.

We all desire the freedom to spend our time in any way we choose. Make full use of your time and make ever second count. Don't bother spending your time and attention on trivial matters. Your time is too precious to spend trying to please everyone. Your loved ones are most deserving of your time. They relieve you from the worries and frustrations of day-to-day routines.

Priorities, Priorities

What we don't want is a situation where we get so caught up with other matters that we neglect spending time with those who are in need of our time and attention. If you get your priorities mixed up, your closest family will be the first to be affected. I have experienced this myself on many occasions in the past. There was a point in time when I occupied my time and attention with so much external issues that I find myself frequently coming home in a horrible mood. I'd quarrel with my wife over the most pettiest things and I would be quick to get angry at my kids. I soon realized this pattern but I had no idea what was the source of my frustrations. After much reflection only then I realized that it was these 'external issues' which was draining a HUGE amount of my time, energy and attention.

I was obssessed over these external issues which had absolutely little to no impact on my quality of life whatsover. Some examples I can remember were:

1. My job
2. My in-laws
3. My siblings' affairs
4. My friends' problems

It is very important to take note of what you can change and what you cannot change. For these examples I have listed above, they are matters which are of relatively low importance, compared to my health, my family's well-being and my own self-development. But yet I invested a huge amount of time into them—and it compromised the quality of my family life. I had no choice but to stop and reassess my priorities. And it instantly turned my life around.

Also, think about the people you used to know who have passed away. For some they have died naturally, and others may have been taken from us unexpectedly in tragic fashion. Either way, I'm sure if given a chance they would want to come back and be given a second chance to spend their life more constructively. Unfortunately, we only have one chance. Their time may be up for them, but as long as you're still living and breathing, you have the opportunity to make your life worthwhile.

Do you really think there is a 'right time' for you to start making a difference? Think again.

Chapter 8:
The Dangers of Assuming

Quit Making Assumptions

To 'ASSUME' is to make an 'ASS' out of 'U' and 'ME'!

I love sharing this quote because it is so true. Base all your decisions on your assumptions and trust me, you'll lead a horrible life. Many of us fill our minds with unnecessary worries because we tend to assume things about our spouses (*they must be seeing someone else*), our friends (*they're out enjoying without me*), our children (*they're up to no good*), our colleagues (*they're talking about me*), etc. Any of these thoughts sound familiar?

Of all these assumptions, the assumption that people are talking about you behind your back can really take a toll on your mental health. Quit assuming people are assuming stuff about you! Do what you set your mind to do, and if you make mistakes—it's up to you how you handle it.

Assuming may seem harmless but it actually leads you to think and see the worse of others, and that creates a negative energy in you. You may not realize this but negative energy is very contagious. It can be easily transferred as it is absorbed. You may have absorbed all this bad energy from negative people or negative surroundings.

Hence it's always wise to choose friends who are positive and who empower you.

The more you harbour ill intentions towards others, the more you build up the negative energy within you. And you'll find that your life is nothing short of miserable. I made the conscious decision to stop concerning myself with the affairs of other people in my life because I realize that it brings absolutely no benefit. Instead I chose to focus on how I can be better and how I can add more value to the lives of others. Now I frequently find myself discussing with my family and friends ideas on how to be better in terms of wealth, skill, knowledge and relationships. This is possible because I surround myself with equally positive and motivated people who wish to improve themselves as well.

The idea is simple: negative thoughts attract a negative reality.

The Worse Ways To Spend Your Life

I used to invest a huge amount of time and energy talking about other people. I lived a life where I constantly assumed the worse in people even though they were completely baseless and unrealistic. When you spread false rumours about a person, it is the same as lying. You're only slandering based on your own judgments and assumptions—creating more unhealthy negative energy for yourself. Eventually you burn out from all the pent up stress you create inside yourself.

Never, ever speak ill of anyone because it will ultimately derail you from becoming successful. It blinds you from the truly important things in life. **Focus on what matters, starting with YOUR OWN LIFE and the people you love and who love you.**

Time waits for no man, and you'll never be able to get back the time you have lost. In creating a better life for ourselves, time is of the essence. You can't afford to waste a second on things which drain and distract you. In order to bring in more positivity and eliminate negativity, we have to start becoming more aware of our own behaviours. Here are some negative behaviours you should avoid at all costs:

1. Backbiting
2. Gossiping
3. Slandering
4. Blaming
5. Cheating
6. Lying
7. Complaining
8. Unhealthy competition
9. Bragging
10. And of course, ASSUMING

Doing any of the above will not do you or anyone else any good. They are like poison whereby the antidote is a little dose of everyday positivity. Start to see the good in every situation. Don't try to look for happiness, just BE happy!

If you want to change the reality you are experiencing, you have to start with changing what you are doing. I'm not expecting you to become a completely different person in a day, so don't feel guilty when you find yourself gossiping. However, do be more aware of these dangerous patterns because they take a toll on your happiness and overall well-being.

The Story of A Repentant Murderer

I'd like to share with you the story of a murderer who had killed 999 men. One day the murderer felt repentant and went to see a wise old saint. He asked the saint whether God will forgive him after killing 999 men. The saint vehemently objected, so out of habit, the murderer killed him. The murderer, now even more dejected from his actions, went to see another saint, who was wiser than the previous one. He asked the saint, "I've now killed a thousand men, if i repent now, would I be forgiven?" The saint calmly replied, "I am uncertain if I have the heart to forgive you. But do not ever despair and lose hope on the mercy of God who is so vast that if you were to come to Him genuinely repentant after killing a thousand more, He would still forgive you." The murderer broke down in tears out of sheer happiness from the sage's comments. He died a repented man.

The moral of the story is simple. No matter how many sins you have committed in the past, if you sincerely try to make amends for your mistakes, God will help you and will send you help along the way. No one is perfect, so you will make more mistakes in the future. But if you move forward with the philosophy of 'You Can Only Be Better', you will eventually find the answers you seek.

All transition starts off uncomfortable but with consistency and belief, it gets easier over time. Remember the dangers of assuming—always seek clarification before making a decision. Never assume something that is not confirmed. In business it can get complicated, especially when you're closing sales. I've been in sales for more than 15 years and when I first start out, I'd assume the client is not interested before I even tried. The deadliest mistake you can do is to start judging before you've established the facts. Our assumptions are usually never true because they are biased on our emotions, senses and experiences. If you assume something based on your own perspective, then you are doomed for failure. At the end of the day, what you focus on will expand and eventually it will come true.

Beware of your own assumptions, assess the facts and make informed decisions. And if you slip up, get back up and be better.

Chapter 9:
Knowledge & Wisdom

Going Straight To The Source

We're living in the information age where access to knowledge is unlimited. With so many avenues for knowledge, how do you know what kind of knowledge to look for? Which school is the best? And how high do we have to be qualified to guarantee a great career future? The fact is our economy is always in a state of flux. The turmoil never ceases and there is nothing is ever guaranteed in the corporate world. You may argue that you have a safety net by hanging onto your certifications, what you've learnt 5 years ago may possibly become irrelevant today. So how do we handle this problem?

Successful people are known not to limit their knowledge to only a few sources. Successful people know that every individual—from the Nobel Prize winning professor to the low-wage janitor—can offer you insights which may enlighten you in ways you can never imagine. I believe regardless of the person or his status, every experience can be a gem of wisdom if you open up your mind and be humble. In every field of knowledge there will be experts who will be more than willing to help you and give you advice. All you need to do, is ask.

For example, if you have a heart condition—seek a heart specialist and not just a General Practitioner. Go straight to the expert and you will have an easier time finding a solution. A General Practitioner may take time to conduct tests on you to define your condition, but the heart specialist would be able to identify your problem in a matter of minutes.

I can't deny that books are one of the greatest sources of knowledge. But my favourite source of knowledge is straight from the mind of the expert himself. As such, I believe attending lessons, seminars and conferences are incredible ways to expand your mind and enrich yourself with ideas. Reading words from an article can never capture your imagination and attention as powerfully as being in person listening to the heartfelt stories told from the author himself.

You will see that learning directly from a teacher or mentor will not just give you new ideas but also fuel the inspiration you need to emulate their success.

For example if you are a huge fan of a certain music artiste, would you be contented to just listening to their songs or would you go to their concert and hear them live? What motivates you to fork out a sum of money to attend their concerts? It's because of the energy. The energy you receive from listening to their songs on your device is nowhere near listening to them perform the songs in a huge auditorium, and definitely much different from just reading their song lyrics.

Being at a concert, you are immersed in the experience with all your senses and you are surrounded with the people who love the performers just as much as you do. This is why I'm a big advocate of going to talks and seminars to gain knowledge. It's definitely worth every penny because not only will you surround yourself with a whole network of people who want success as much as you do, you will supercharge your desire and positivity to a whole new level.

The Four Stages of Wisdom

A business veteran battle-hardened by trials and tribulations of 40 years in the corporate industry will see life differently from a 21-year old boy fresh out of college. Their words make an impact, their ideas are the driving force of industries. But regardless of age, I believe every successful man in every craft goes through 4 phases before he achieves what we can genuinely call 'wisdom'.

1. Knowledge (The Novice)

Everyone has to start somewhere. When you are introduced to a new idea or concept, you have begun the process of gaining knowledge. But this knowledge is like raw material, like ore dug up from the mines, still unprocessed. It is the most surface level of knowledge where you have yet to make sense of the information you have just obtained. At this first stage, you have to ask as many questions as possible so that you can maximize your understanding.

2. Understanding (The Apprentice)

And that brings me to the next stage of wisdom, that is understanding the knowledge. You now have a firm grasp of the knowledge and you can competently summarize or teach the principles to others. However, this stage should never be mistaken as wisdom. Imagine you're asking for marketing advice from your business lecturer in college who has been teaching the concepts for years but had never marketed anything in his life before. Would you call him an expert? Being in the academic faculty, he would only be able to explain to you the theory of marketing but can never accurately tell you how effective his principles are in real life. Likewise, a historian of WW2 can give you a detailed recount of the events of the war but his stories can never be as graphic and visceral as a war veteran who was actually there fighting in the trenches.

3. Experience (The Journeyman)

Experience is the real prerequisite to wisdom. Why doers usually grow faster than talkers is simply because of experience. When you actually apply your knowledge, you get will get feedback. When you have feedback, you are able to make an informed decision on how to improve yourself. You get experience when Back in ancient times, apprentices will study under the mentorship of their masters for years before the master will allow them to further honing their craft in the outside world. When they set off on their journey, they know that their road to mastery is just beginning.

4. Wisdom (The Master)

Wisdom is immeasurable. A wise man will never claim himself to be an expert because he is never satisfied with his current level of knowledge. Wisdom is achieved after one has gone through years of experiences, both sweet and bitter. Masters will definitely know first hand the sweetness of triumph, and the long periods of struggle frustration it takes to get there. There is no easy path to wisdom. It comes in time when one dedicates his life to the mastery of his craft.

People of Wisdom

Seek out people of wisdom because they will be able to make the greatest impact on your life. They may speak a few words but their words carry immense weight and meaning—a testament of their remarkable experience. You can immediately feel the sincerity in their words and find yourself relating their ideas to your own situation. I definitely have felt many 'aha' moments listening to such people and I'd realize exactly where I went wrong in the past. Most great mentors will share from the heart and genuinely wants you to be successful in life. **If they are sincere you will feel it in your heart, because you can never fake true wisdom.**

Sitting with these mentors and spending time with them is one of the surefire ways to accelerate your success in any field. Their presence and ideas are enough to make you feel smarter, even if you were just sitting down for a 15 minute chat over coffee. No matter how bad your situation, they will be able to bring you out of the darkness and into the light, and lead you to the answers you have been searching for.

The Importance of Lowering Your Ego

The most important thing you need to know before you start learning anything is to LOWER YOUR EGO. Never ever assume that you know everything there is to know about a particular subject. Knowledge can be absorbed only after you have wholeheartedly admitted: 'Yes I do not know, please teach me." **If you want to reach the highest level of knowledge that is wisdom, you have to consciously set your mind to focus all attention on learning, so that you can subconsciously eliminate all obstacles in your path.** Just like a ship that has to navigate past icebergs in its way, you need the guidance of an experienced captain as well as enough resources to last you in your journey.

We all need mentors for every area in our life. Because they have gone through a certain series of experiences, they can see what we fail to see. Therefore they can give us a better perspective on our current reality and the direction we are heading. They know which pitfalls to look out for and what dangers to avoid—because they experienced the consequences first-hand. They may seem so flawless in their presence and performance that you would never have imagined that they started out just like you and me. They too, started out incompetent—struggling to make ends meet, shouldering mountains of debt, shedding tears of frustration trying to get it right. Today they are enjoying the rewards because they never gave up and never stopped learning new things.

Humility is essential in the path to greater knowledge. What we know is but a tiny drop of water from a vast ocean. Human beings will always make new discoveries. The more we think we know, the more we have yet to discover. Even now with the internet revolution, the playing field can change within a split second. Technology can create jobs and opportunities and can just as easily take them away from us in favour of automated machines. There are pros and cons to every solution and it never hurts to always have an expert opinion on our current situation.

Never Stop Learning

As you reflect on the value of knowledge, think about just how much time you have left to gain knowledge. Do you think you would have made better decisions in the past if you had the knowledge? No matter how much we wish it sometimes, we can't rewind our life and restart back over in our mother's womb. The only mother we're ever going back to is Mother Earth! So start looking forward and have the intention to be better.

No matter how much you choose to invest in building your knowledge, you will have nothing to lose. It is the single best investment you can make for yourself—so embark on your own self-development journey and remember to share your knowledge so that others may benefit. That's exactly what I'm doing right now with this book.

Never stop learning. Because what you've learnt today has made you better than who you were yesterday.

Chapter 10:
Living Life With Compassion

Compassion Makes The World Go Round

You can never live your life to the fullest if you're only thinking about yourself. The world belongs to all of us. The man living next door is no different from the man halfway around the world. **As long as we're still breathing, we all possess the same potential and opportunities for abundance as every other person on this planet.**

The world reflects back to us what we give in the first place. Live your life full of compassion and the world responds to you with compassion. Show compassion towards yourself, your family, your neighbours even the animals around you. One reason why people feel stuck in life is because they are so hostile towards the people around them. The same hostility is then reflected back to them and they wonder why their lives are so miserable. The world is round. **Whatever you put out to the world will always come back to you. It is a law of nature.**

In this final chapter, I will talk about probably the most important value in this book: compassion. They say love makes the world go round, right? Well you can't have love without compassion.

Everyone Needs Compassion

There's an old Arabic proverb which says that the strength of a man lies not in his physique but in his ability to control his anger. We are living in a fast paced world where most of us lead our lives waiting our next paycheck, worrying about the unpaid bills and working to put food on the table. On an average day, there'll be a thousand and one reasons to complain about what's not working. We take our anger and frustrations out on the people around us, because we forget that they are humans too. We forget that the people around us need the same respect and appreciation we crave.

We are all in the same boat. We could all use a little bit of compassion from the people around us. But before we can expect to receive compassion, we have to first learn to give it. How? You can start by smiling and wishing them well. A little positivity will brighten a person's day. A little kindness will go a long way.

Many people are unhappy because they are stuck in jobs they absolutely hate. I worked for 17 years in jobs I never enjoyed before I finally called it quits and started my own business. I took a risk and it was worth it, because I now enjoy a new sense of freedom I never had. I'm not asking you to quit. But if you are unhappy with your job, there are steps you can take to start turning your life around.

The Meaning of True Success

Start by first being thankful that unlike millions of people across the globe, you actually HAVE a job. Realize why you are working so hard in the first place—for your family who needs you. Compassion is priceless—so regardless of your financial status, never stop showing compassion. Seek out more ways to help the people around you. Do more acts of kindness. Life

45

gets easier because you choose to make others' lives easier. You make life rewarding for others, and life will reward you in return.

With what you have, always ensure you save a portion to develop yourself. The best investment you can have is your own KNOWLEDGE. **Always, always, always upgrade yourself**. Go read some books, or consult a wise veteran in the industry. If you plan to leave your unforgiving job, why delay any longer? Get off the fence and make a decision now! Would you go for that seminar and take your career to the next level? Or take that leap of faith and start your own business?

My friends, showing love and compassion is essential. There really is no substitute for compassion because without compassion, the world would be a lifeless place to live in. It's always a ripple effect. When you throw a pebble into a pond, ripples are created on the water surface. Positivity is a ripple effect. If you are full of positive energy, you are like the epicentre of a ripple effect—sending waves of positivity to everyone around you. Be a source of compassion, love and happiness and observe the kind of people you attract into your life. Observe how your friends react towards you. Observe how your presence fills their day with joy and warmth.

If you apply the principles taught in this book and adopt the lessons into your own lifestyle, you will begin to see the bigger picture: **that true success comes when your presence adds value to the lives of others**. That's when you will experience a sense of fulfilment. True success will feel truly fulfilling—a feeling you can never achieve when you have a self-centered view on life. People talk about success as having wealth when in reality success is in the GIVING of wealth, or sacrificing the things we value most to benefit the people we love and care for.

Do not judge or belittle anyone. Be kind. Be honest. Be compassionate. These are the characteristics of the successful and the people who are destined for a high standing in society. People who possess these traits go the extra mile in ensuring their time, wealth and efforts are invested in enriching the lives of the people around them.

Because ultimately, what you put out to the world, will always be returned to you multiplied.

I pray that all of you will experience a richer and more fulfilling in your days ahead. No matter where you are in life, it does not matter.

You know you can only be better.

EKONIAGA

RANGSANG MINDA: Syed Muhammad (tengah) sedang berbincang idea bagi program program yang akan dikendalikan dengan dua pelatihnya, Encik Saiful Redzuan Mohammad Nasir (kiri) dan Encik Hyder Muhammad Taufik. - Foto TUKIMAN WARJI

Lega program dapat perhatian CLF

Langkah firma motivasi tukar strategi buahkan hasil lepas berbulan gagal pikat pelanggan

▶ATIYYAH MOHD SAID
atiyyah@bh.com.sg

SETELAH berbulan gagal menarik pelanggan, program mantap semangat kelolaan firma penyedia latihan motivasi belia, The Green Apple Project, menarik perhatian Forum Pemimpin Masyarakat (CLF).

Kini, syarikat yang diasaskan Syed Muhammad Abu Bakar Syed Sharikat Hussain itu akan menerima sokongan CLF Labs dan dibiayai bagi mengendalikan program motivasi bagi golongan berisiko di bawah Mendaki.

The Green Apple Project ditubuhkan tahun lalu, menyusuli pengalaman Syed Muhammad yang mengalami kecederaan teruk dalam satu kemalangan pada 2008.

Selepas meningsikan dunia perniagaan pada 2010 akibat kerugian $60,000 kerana projek luar negara yang tidak menjadi, beliau menubuhkan berniaga semula tahun lalu dengan bantuan isterinya, Cik Fitri Aisyah Akhmal Firdaus, 37 tahun.

Lantaran itu, Syed Muhammad, 36 tahun, menganggap pelantikan firmanya sebagai rakan kerjasama CLF Labs sebagai satu pencapaian besar dan adalah hasil daripada perubahan strategi yang dilakukan.

"Pada awalnya kami tertumpu pada menganjurkan program untuk masyarakat awam dan korporat kerana saya yakin ia satu formula yang akan berjaya memandangkan saya sudah terlibat dalam industri itu hampir 17 tahun. Tetapi

selama berbulan-bulan, kami gagal menarik pelanggan.

"Ini mendorong kami memikirkan semula strategi perniagaan dan sedar bahawa sebenarnya saya ingin membantu mereka yang berisiko. Pengalaman pahit saya yang terpaksa bangkit semula dapat menjadi sumber motivasi kepada orang lain," ujar bapa seorang anak itu.

Di bawah kerjasama dengan CLF, Syed Muhammad menjangkakan perniagaannya akan tumbuh 10 hingga 15 peratus dan sekurang-kurangnya tiga sekolah akan menjadi pelanggannya mulai bulan depan.

Apa yang menarik, firma tersebut tidak menawarkan senarai program yang tetap, tetapi ia membangunkan konsep motivasi asas yang kemudiannya digunakan bagi menghasilkan program khusus yang diingini oleh sekolah-sekolah tersebut.

"Ini akan membezakan kami daripada kebanyakan firma latihan lain kerana permintaan pelanggan adalah pelbagai," tambahnya yang mengepikkan dua pelatih.

About the Author

Syed Muhammad Abu Bakar is the founder and executive director of The Green Apple Project Pte Ltd.

Over 17 years of experience as a director in the corporate world, Syed Muhammad Abu Bakar is exceptionally effective in dealing with people from all walks of life. His talent for engaging others soon cultivated in him a burning passion to speak as a mentor and a coach. After triumphs over many gruelling life challenges, Syed feels strongly compelled to share the most valuable lessons he's learnt with others with the intention to add value to their lives. He has contributed much to organizations and institutes everywhere and they loved his vivacious and humorous delivery of topics at hand. His hope is to educate others on how to navigate through the meanders of life effectively with minimal stress and a value-oriented approach to problem solving.

Today The Green Apple Project is the fastest rising youth inspiration organization in Singapore, after influencing over 2000 youths within its first year. The Green Apple Project specializes in turning youths into self-motivated achievers, passionate learners and dedicated leaders.

As a father of three sons, Syed is a dedicated family man who thrives on the love and passion he shares with his wife and kids.